...we are 1
(Elaine, L
light-hear
and enjoy a good laugh and plenty of family banter.

We want to say right at the start that this book is not for all the clever-clogs out there, who have been cultivating veg for years and know all the neat tricks and dazzling science of the art. It's been written to help those of you who don't know your 'pricking-out' (behave yourselves in the back row) from your 'earthing-up', but fancy having a go at growing things to eat, whether you've got a garden or not and is based on the crash course in veg growing that Elaine wrote for our blog last spring.

One more thing – the rewards of growing your own veg are many, but you may get lots of failures too. We all do (Caroline, more than most, obviously!) But we hope above all, that you ENJOY the thrill of growing food and end up with a wonderful and absorbing hobby for life.

If we have whetted your appetite for more from us, please go to the3growbags.com, and sign up to receive our weekly gardening blog – we would LOVE to have you onboard!

Caroline (left), Elaine and Laura taking one of the innumerable breaks required by gardeners. The cake can only just be out of shot.

Foreword by Fern Britton

Author and Broadcaster

The vegetable garden was formerly considered a very male preserve but now everyone's having a go!

And let's be honest, female gardeners do have a knack of introducing a different sort of harmony and a softness to the practical business of growing food for the table.

Whatever gender, new veg gardeners tend not to be afraid to experiment and there's no limit to the new colours, shapes and tastes you can produce from a plot or a pot.

You don't need a big garden, or even a garden at all for that matter, to enjoy some home-grown freshness and to bring a new joie de vivre to your kitchen.

It's never too late to start and The3Growbags are here to help you succeed!

Contents

1. The veg bed and other matters.......................... 7
2. Potatoes 11
3. Broad beans 15
4. Onions 19
5. Dwarf runner beans, peas and carrots............ 23
6. Tomatoes 27
7. Salads... 31
8. Courgettes and squashes................................ 35
9. Winter veg.. 39
10. Chard, spinach and kale................................ 43
11. Fruit 47
12. Herbs... 51

1. The veg bed and other matters

First of all a few little pointers for the novice veg grower

1. WHERE:

A vegetable bed should ideally be in a sunny place, away from big trees and hedges. If you only have a shady corner, it's still possible to grow things like lettuce, peas and spinach. Having a source of water close by is a real advantage. Buying or making raised beds is a fabulous idea if you can, for ease of control and access.

A large water container fed from a gutter, with a lid into which you can dip watering cans can be a great help. If you don't have a garden, then you can still grow plenty in pots in a sunny porch or perhaps on a balcony. No outdoor space at all? Well pea-shoots, micro-greens, even chillies and tomatoes will grow perfectly well on a sunny windowsill.

2. SIZE:

The bigger the patch, the more things you can grow generally, but if you only have a metre-square to play with, you can still grow lots of lovely stuff to eat.

A sunny bit of lawn can make a great veg patch

It is fantastically helpful for your plants if you can tend them all without walking on the soil (which damages its structure, especially in wet weather). In a big area, allow for paths alongside your veg, and if you must walk on the soil, try to use a plank which spreads your weight more evenly.

3. HOW:

If you're nicking a bit of lawn, mark out your plot, then take off the turf. (If you can stack the taken-off turves upside down somewhere in a corner of the garden for a year, they turn into the most AWESOME topsoil!)

Dig over your chosen patch of soil. If it's ghastly: solid clay, chalk, etc. then digging in some compost or manure, or grit (for clay) at this stage, will hugely increase your chances of good crops. Break up the top layer using a spade, hoe, rake etc. The aim is to end up with a covering of fine soil ('tilth' – there's a great word!) over at least a foot (30cm) of good useable soil.

4. ONGOING:

Vigilance must be your watchword. We now acknowledge we were doing untold harm to the environment and the food chain by using hundreds of chemicals to treat garden problems in the past. To save our crops by gentler means (e.g. jets of water to wash off aphids, coffee grounds to deter slugs etc.), we need to be 'on it' much more quickly. The line goes 'The shadow of the gardener is the best fertilizer'.

Watering:
Watering deeply at the roots (not on the leaves) two to three times a week, is far better than a small trickle each day, which encourages the roots up to the surface where they can fry on hot days. Watering is of course critically important for plants in pots – some smaller pots and hanging baskets are likely to need watering every day in dry weather. Water in the early morning or early evening for preference, to lessen the threat of evaporation.

Weeding:
Stay on top of this; weeds are going to enjoy all this pampering as much as your plants are, so weeding little and often is the best way. Above all, don't let them flower and set seed – 'One year's seeding, seven year's weeding' is how the old adage goes...

Don't forget to label everything!

Labelling:
You always think you're going to remember what you planted where...but you won't. Especially label any rows of seeds you've sown. The birds rather like pecking out the little labels, by the way, so keep checking they're still in place.

Companion planting:
This is a technique that involves growing plants together to help reduce pest attack, improve pollination, provide extra nutrients, or support, etc. For instance, I have pots of mint in the greenhouse (never grow it in the veg plot soil or it will completely take over!) and the scent deters whitefly.

Lots of herbs – lavender, rosemary, thyme, sage, borage – growing among your vegetables can attract pollinators (good) as well as deter pests. And nasturtiums will lure blackfly away from your broad beans. It all makes the veg patch or pot look pretty too!

Seeds:
On the subject of seeds and seedlings, it's just worth giving a few basic principles:

a) They germinate at different times — might seem obvious, but I'm just asking you not to give up on them too soon. It's always worth sowing a few more a little bit later if the first seeds don't do anything.
b) Never sow your seed thickly — it makes for weakened seedlings and a lot of wastage.
c) A sunny windowsill will work for most seeds that have to be started inside. A propagator, a sheet of glass or a plastic bag fixed over the pot and taken off every so often to allow aeration, will help seeds that require a bit more warmth.
d) 'Prick out' the seedlings from the seed tray into their own modules as soon as you can loosen the roots and lift them safely by their leaves without touching their delicate stems.
e) Always 'thin' seedlings to the recommended distance apart, or the crowding and competition for nutrients will result in a much-inferior crop for you.

2. Potatoes

Spuds are a fabulous thing for veg beginners! And you can grow them in almost anything...

1. CHOOSING VARIETIES:

So many varieties from which to choose

Buying your seed potatoes can be confusing, because there are so many different categories — 'First Earlies', 'Maincrop' etc. Keep things simple if you're a novice. And don't buy too many — they make big plants — about 1 foot (30cm) all round! How about going for something straightforward like Arran Pilot (a First Early) or Maris Piper (Main Crop)? Or choose something that you can't usually get in the shops, like the quaintly-named Pink Fir Apple — an oddly-shaped but delicious salad potato that is a particular favourite with The3growbags...

It is possible to grow potatoes from a bag of supermarket spuds, indeed you'll often see sprouts coming from bought potatoes in your kitchen veg drawer in early spring. The danger is they aren't guaranteed to be free of viruses or a disease called 'blackleg' in the same way as proper seed potatoes. And they may also have been treated with a bud-suppressant. If you do want to have a go at growing supermarket potatoes, I strongly suggest growing them in a container of some sort rather than out in the open garden, so you can control what happens a bit more.

2. CHITTING:

Once you have your seed potatoes, you can do one of two things:

Plant them out straight away any time from the last two weeks in March until about the end of April. **Or.**

Pop each one on a sunny windowsill for a week or two (empty egg-boxes are handy to put them in) to develop some strong stubby shoots ('chits') before you plant them out in the soil. This is what I do, because I like to know which way to plant them in the soil (chit-side up!)

Another nifty advantage to doing this 'chitting', is that if your seed potatoes are quite large, and you can see sprouts developing on several sides, you can cut the spud into halves or even quarters. As long as each bit of potato has a sprout or two, it will grow independently!

Chitting your seed potatoes

3. PLANTING:

A good sunny spot is best, though they can tolerate a bit of shade. The thing to remember about timing is that potatoes will take about four weeks before they start to appear above ground, and even a touch of frost can damage the foliage. A severe frost can kill them completely. You know when the last frost is generally expected in your area, so plant your spuds four weeks earlier than that. (The average for the UK is the end of April, so plant your seed spuds at the end of March). It's not an exact science – some gardeners always plant their potatoes on Easter Sunday, whenever that may fall.

Make shallow trenches 1 foot (30cm) apart, and place your seed potatoes 1 foot (30cm) apart along the bottom of the trench, cover them with soil, and water the row.

If you don't have space for a veg bed, you can grow spuds in all sorts of containers as well – big pots, specialised potato-bags, supermarket bags-for-life, plastic compost bags with the top chopped off and most of the compost taken out, even bags made from stapling together weed-suppressing fabric... Just make sure you have plenty of drainage holes in any container you use. Three seed potatoes per container would be about right. Put a little compost in the bottom, add the potatoes then just cover them with compost, leaving plenty of room at the top to add more later.

4. EARTHING UP:

This peculiar business involves piling the soil up around the stems as they grow, which forces new potatoes to form above the ones you planted. Start doing this about five weeks after you planted them, and then do it again at weekly intervals, if you can remember. Some gardeners cover all the foliage completely each time, but I like to keep a tuft of growth out of the top, so I can tell when they are ready to harvest.

Keep your tatties well-watered; and a bit of liquid fertiliser won't go amiss if you can manage it, every couple of weeks.

5. HARVESTING:

Most types of potatoes are ready to be harvested about five months after they were planted. That's

Potato shoots

the middle-to-end of August in most cases. Quite a lot of spuds can be big enough to eat after only about 10 weeks, but you'll get a much larger crop by leaving them longer.

Once the leaves turn yellow and begin to die back, you'll know it's time to leave them in the ground for one more fortnight, then dig them up.

DON'T use a spade for this – you'll heartbreakingly slice through too many tubers that way. Use a garden fork very carefully to loosen the soil, then plunge your hands in to retrieve your gorgeous spuds.

6. STORAGE:

Never keep potatoes in a plastic bag (they sweat and rot – lovely!). Use paper sacks, and store them in a cool dark place. In the light, they'll go green and become poisonous.

I can't promise it'll all be plain sailing – even the best gardeners sometimes have to deal with the odd slug or blight attack... but the good old spud is generally a dependable and delicious stalwart.

3. Broad beans

I love growing my own broad beans because they are SO seasonal! They're one of the few things you can only buy fresh in supermarkets at certain times of the year.

And simply delectable whether you eat the beans whole when young or shucked of their tough skins when they're bigger.

1. CHOOSING SEEDS:

There are lots of varieties of broad bean to choose from, with fabulous names like Imperial Green Long Pod and Crimson Flowered (these are pretty as well!). Bunyard's Exhibition is a tried and tested variety for a beginner and The Sutton is a good one to go for if you're growing your beans in pots (perfectly feasible in a sunny spot) or are limited for space, because they don't grow so tall.

2. PLANTING:

Broad beans are tough old things (much like us Growbags!) and lots of gardeners like to plant some seeds in the autumn to get an early crop the following year – even as early as May. But it's fine to plant them even in late spring – they're really fast growers once they get the bit between their teeth. If you can sprinkle a bit of fertiliser on the soil so much the better, but you don't need anything that says it's high in nitrogen, because broad bean plants are full of it, anyway!

I usually get my broad beans going in cardboard loo-roll innards or rather fancier root-trainer modules before planting them out into the veg patch, but you don't have to. I do this because I like to know beforehand which seeds are duff and therefore don't need a space on my bamboo support-frame. Another thing you can do to find this out is to soak the seeds for a day or so in plain water, wrap them in damp kitchen roll, stick them a plastic bottle and close the lid. Put the bottle somewhere warm and check the seeds after about four days to see if they've germinated (got little roots growing). Laura uses this method for her sweet pea seeds, using Tupperware containers.

Important! Get your support structure in place BEFORE you plant your beans, especially if you're growing them in a large pot. They're definitely going to need tying in to something as they grow, and because they grow so quickly it is much harder to put in bamboo canes or trellis or whatever after they've already started flopping. A wigwam of canes can work well and is more stable than single canes. I make a double row of slanted canes tied together with a couple of cross-canes for strength, and there is about 10 inches (25cm) between the two rows.

Water the soil where you're going to plant, and place your seeds, germinated or not, 2 inches (5cm) deep, and 8-10 inches (20-25cm) apart. If you haven't germinated them, find the dark spot on each one (actually called an 'eye') and have that at the bottom of your seed. Some gardeners actually bung two seeds at each point, to allow for some of them not germinating at all! I reckon three seeds to a big pot would be about right. Water again.

3. GROWING ON:

Broad beans can tolerate a bit of dryness but they HATE drying out completely. The best thing to do is water deeply (the soil around them, not the plants themselves) either first thing in the morning or in the evening, daily in hot weather.

Pinch out the tops of broad beans

Tie in the stems as they shoot upwards using soft twine, string, wool, anything like that. Never use wire which will break the stems.

Please be careful about weeding them. They have frighteningly shallow roots and take it from me, it's horribly easy to damage them when you are poking about uprooting a dandelion..........

When you see pods starting to appear after the flowers near the bottom of the bean stems, pinch out the top of each plant between your thumb and forefinger, or snip it off. This will encourage it to stop producing more leaves and put its energy into bean-production – hooray!

Also pinch out the tops of any plants that become infested with black-fly or aphids. (A couple of other tips here, if you encounter this common problem – spray these little sap-suckers with a water-jet to hose them off, or grow some nasturtiums nearby, and hope the beasties get lured away from your precious beans...If you get white spots on the leaves and they start to crinkle up, this is mildew. Cut out the affected bits, and make sure you never wet the leaves when you're watering; this problem can be worse if your plants are very crowded together.

4. HARVESTING:

You can pick some of the pods when they are still small. You can even pick them before they've got beans visible in them, and eat the whole pod steamed like sugar snap peas. You might find though, that they don't have as much flavour as they do later. I prefer to wait until we see the beans bulging in the pods, but not so late that they are looking dry. Keep picking (snip off the pods rather than pulling them) to keep the plant producing more flowers and thus more beans.

Bees sometimes cheat and pierce the back of the flower to get to the nectar

4. Onions

Here's the most versatile vegetable of them all. Not usually difficult, unless you live in a swamp, and lovely to have on hand at almost any time in the kitchen.

1. SEEDS, SETS, ONIONS AND SHALLOTS:

You can grow onions from seed, which is a cheaper option, but many gardeners, and certainly beginners, prefer to grow them from immature bulbs, known as 'sets', being more likely to mature quickly, especially if you live in chilly parts of the country, and frankly much less of a fuss than seeds.

Your choices include the big Spanish types of milder onion like 'Ailsa Craig', the smaller stronger ones like 'Sturon', or red ones like 'Red Baron'. I usually go for shallots which are the easiest of the lot to grow, and have a mild, sweet almost garlicky taste. They grow differently – an onion set turns into a bigger onion, a shallot set turns into a cluster of small shallots attached to a base and each with its own papery skin. 'Golden Gourmet' is a well-known variety, but there are lots of others, just as nice.

2. PLANTING:

I always plant my onions or shallots in late March. It's perfectly possible to plant onion sets in the autumn – you might get earlier and heavier crops that way. But what they *really* don't like is the wet.

You need a good sunny place – in pots or window-boxes, if that's what you've got available, or a raised bed if you have such a thing (a good way of making sure they sit in well-drained soil). Onions positively dislike manured soil. They might be happy with a bit of general fertiliser sprinkled over, but definitely not one that's high in nitrogen.

Put your sets into the soil along a nice neat row, 4-6 inches (10-15cm) apart, and a foot (30cm) between rows if you have more than one. Plant them with their little papery noses just showing above the soil.

Now we come to something that is very endearing but also rather annoying – our precious native birds are tempted to pull up the little straw-like tops as potential nesting material, and you come back to find your babies

Grow onions at the surface of soil

scattered all over the shop! Slinging a net over them until they are growing strongly is one option.

There's another way to fool them – if you plant your sets in modules of compost first and keep them protected and moist for a week or so, they'll develop green shoots and, more importantly, roots. Then you can plant them in your intended place outside, and the roots will anchor them more firmly in the ground when the blackbirds and pigeons come calling. Lovely!

3. GROWING ON:

Caring for your growing onions is really very simple. They like things sunny and on the dry side, but do water them in hot spells. Their roots are shallow and easily damaged so be very careful with a hoe, or better still, hand-weed them.

There's another reason for weeding them with care – if you do damage a root or two, the plant thinks it might die soon and immediately starts trying to send up a flowering shoot! This is called 'bolting' and onions and shallots are rather prone to doing it, I'm afraid. Funny weather, a weed growing too close to them, the gardener looking too smug... and they think, 'right, that's it, I'm on the way out, I'd better propagate myself RIGHT NOW!' This will cause your lovely onion to go all woody and inedible, so if you see it happening, whip off the flowering stem right away, and see what you can salvage of the bulb. Some suppliers sell heat-treated sets which prevent them from bolting, but they are usually more expensive.

Other than that, onions are pretty easy. Yes, you MIGHT get a visitation from nasties like onion fly or white rot etc. just be vigilant and 'oik' out any that look sickly. But by and large, onions and shallots are a piece of cake!

4. HARVESTING:

Onion and shallot sets planted in March should be ready by the beginning of August roughly, but it does all depend on where you live, of course, how hot the summer is etc. They'll tell you they're ready for harvesting by drooping and browning their leaves, but you can also pick them earlier than that if you want to and they look big enough.

Scoop round them with a trowel and unearth them gently, and then they need a period of drying out in the sun, either on the top of the soil or some other sunny place, with all their roots and leaves still on, quietly withering away.

5. STORAGE:

After a couple of weeks, tidy them up, and store them hanging in a string bag in an airy, dry, cool, place. They'll be fine and ready for use in the kitchen for months and months. If you spot any that have grey mould growing on them, get them out straight away or the mould will spread to others. What is even more fun, is to string them together – it's easy to do, and it's what I do with mine every year.

Leave harvested onions to dry in a sunny place

5. Dwarf runner beans, peas and carrots

Peas and beans can grow like the clappers so they're a really good type of veg to try if you're new to it all...

1. DWARF FRENCH/RUNNER BEANS:

Dwarf beans are brilliant because they don't need all the faffing about with supports that taller runner beans need! March is the perfect time to sow these lovelies because the soil has warmed up a bit. Great for growing in pots, too.

Sow the seeds indoors into compost in individual modules or little pots about 2 inches (4cm) deep. Water with tepid water, but don't keep the compost permanently wet, or your seed may rot. Leave them to germinate on a windowsill – it takes between a week and a fortnight usually.

They'll grow quite quickly and may need moving into slightly larger pots, but don't put them outside permanently until they've been 'hardened' off i.e. put outside for a short while each day to get acclimatised to cooler air, and brought in at night. Slowly leave them out for longer and longer. They can't take any frost, but should be ready to stay in their outdoor space by the end of May in most parts of the country.

Plant them in a warm, sheltered place and in light soil, with 6-9 inches (15-22cm) between plants, and 18 inches (45cm) between rows. Use a similar spacing if you're growing them in a pot. Some twiggy sticks might help them to stay upright. And watch out for slugs! Put down organic slug bait or make beer-traps for them – pots of beer round your plants that are sunk into the ground. The beasties fall into them and then drown... not everyone's preferred solution.

Harvesting should begin by the middle to end of July. Keep on picking them to encourage more to form. If you want dried beans for the winter months, chop the plants down in September and hang the stems upside-down to dry in the sun. When the pods are crispy-dry, pop out the beans and store them in an airtight container to use in stews. And maybe save a few to sow next year as well.

Dwarf runner beans will grow in a trug with drainage holes!

2. PEAS/PEASHOOTS:

There's nothing like the freshness and sweetness of peas straight from the pod!

They don't usually need mollycoddling or lots of fertiliser but aren't happy on chilly, wet soils. And they are super to grow in pots or patio bags as well as in the veg patch.

Make a flat trench about 2 inches (5cm) deep and 6 inches (15cm) wide in your chosen spot. Sow your seed evenly along your trench, about 3 inches (7-8cm) apart. Cover them with soil and firm them in. Use the same spacing and depth if you're sowing into a pot. Some netting is a good idea, to keep the birds off. Sow more in about a fortnight's time, and then again a fortnight after that. Water the area, and they should germinate in a couple of weeks at most.

Give them something to scramble up – netting, trellis, canes or string etc. Water them more when you start to see flowers and harvest the pods regularly to keep them producing more.

VERY short of space? Try growing pea-shoots in a little tray. You can even do this during the winter indoors – peas are one of

Pea-shoots in a sunny window!

the few veg crops that don't need huge amounts of sun. Almost any container will do, as long as it has drainage holes in the bottom. During the Summer, it will be fine outside in a shady spot, or inside in a cool place.

Fill it with compost, water it, and sow your seeds close together over the top. Cover with half an inch of compost, firm it down, and keep the compost moist. Start harvesting your delectable pea-shoots in about three weeks. Sow a few every five days or so for a continuous supply.

3. CARROTS:

Carrots are great in pots! They can be very choosy as to soil (not stony, not heavy, not too acid or alkaline, not too dry, blah, blah). Critters attack them when they are out in the veg patch – eelworms, carrot root fly... (I don't think it is JUST me!) But when they are growing in a pot, planter, window-box, tub etc., you can control all of those things. If your chosen container is at least 12 inches (30cm) deep, you can grow almost any variety of carrot. If it's shorter than that, then go for shorter varieties like 'Chantenay' or 'Nantes' or even some of the miniature 'Amsterdam' kinds.

Use a 'light' compost mixture. Add perlite, vermiculite or sand to the mix, if you have any. Water the soil then sprinkle some of your seeds over the surface and cover with a fine layer of compost. The pot should be in a sunny, sheltered spot. Sow more in different containers each week for a month.

Water the pot regularly once you see the seed has germinated and as soon as the plants are 2 inches (5cm) tall, pull out some to leave about 4 inches (10cm) between each one. Try not to disturb the roots of the ones you're leaving in when you do this – the smell of the baby carrots tends to attract the attention of a very tiresome pest called Carrot Root Fly.

Make sure the soil stays right over the growing root or it goes all green and bitter at the top. You should be pulling your first proper carrots about two and a half months from sowing them.

6. Tomatoes

You say tomatoes, I say terrific! They're fabulous for growing in pots, as well as greenhouses and veg plots, and you can even have little varieties like 'Tumbling Tom' in hanging baskets.

A common way of growing them is in growbags (proper ones, not three slightly barmy sisters talking about horticulture amongst other things!), but sunny patios are great, even bay windows indoors...

1. VARIETIES:

As you'll know from the supermarket salad aisles, there are a great many varieties of tomato out there. And that is only a FRACTION of the ones you could grow. The traditional large golf-ball size is represented by old favourites such as 'Moneymaker', which are okay, though some of them can taste a bit 'soggy tennis-ball-ish' unless you're eating them straight off the plant.

The big beefsteak kinds are lovely for hearty salads and summer dishes but can be a little trickier to grow, I find. My preference is for the cherry tomatoes like 'Sungold', 'Gardener's Delight', 'Alicante' or 'Sweet Aperitif'. They're generally easy to grow, more resistant to a nasty disease called tomato blight and delicious for the kitchen.

2. SEED-SOWING:

February and March are the usual months to sow tomato seeds although you can still sow them a bit later and enjoy a good harvest in the summer. Fill a little pot with compost, firm it down and water it. Scatter a FEW seeds over the surface, and cover them with a thin layer of compost or better still, vermiculite or fine grit.

Put the pot on a sunny windowsill and seedlings should start to come up in about a fortnight.

3. PRICKING OUT AND POTTING ON:

Once the seedlings are large enough to handle by holding their leaves, gently unearth them using a little dibber – a pencil is fine, actually – trying not to touch the stem or roots, just the leaves. Move each seedling into its own pot or module of compost ('pricking out'), and grow them on, still inside, until their roots are coming through the drainage holes.

Some gardeners like to strengthen the stems by having a bit of air blowing round them – perhaps a fan going? – to imitate an outdoor breeze. I like to stroke my hand over them for the same reason – and they already have a little of that sharp delectable smell!

Sow seeds in February or March

Pot them on into bigger pots, and at this point, it's really helpful to bury the stems in compost right up to the bottom set of leaves. This makes your plants grow more roots which will feed the plant, and help it become more stable.

If you live in a cold spot, it may be best to grow your toms in a sunny porch, front window, greenhouse etc. If you're going to grow them out of doors, gradually accustom them to the fresher conditions by leaving them out during the day and bringing them in at night. Don't plant them out in the soil until all danger of frost is over in your area. Put canes into the ground as supports before you start planting.

4. GROWING ON:

Unless your tomato packet says your variety is specifically a 'bush' tomato, you're aiming for tomatoes grown on one stem. If you allow a lot of leafy shoots to grow, the plant is having so much fun it can forget that it's supposed to be growing tomatoes!

Loosely tie in the main stem as it grows with soft twine, every 4-6 inches (10-15cm), and watch out for little shoots that grow out from just above each leaf. Snip these off or pinch them out, and your tomato plant will be encouraged to keep heading upwards, setting little trusses of flowers, and therefore fruit, as it goes.

Watering is important, and one way of ensuring it gets to the roots is to sink plant pots into the compost near your tomato plants and fill them up with water daily, early in the morning, or in the evening.

Once the flowers have begun to show on the little branches coming out from the main stem ('trusses'), start feeding your plants with tomato fertiliser once a week. This is high in phosphorus, perfect for most flowering plants, actually. Also, start taking off the bottom leaves below the bottom truss – they start to look a bit manky anyway, and they are the first to show signs of fungal disease.

Tomatoes certainly can get a range of problems, including blight which manifests itself as brown patches on the leaves and stems and fatally weakens the plant. If you see a few tell-tale patches, try and slow its progress by removing and destroying the affected bits. Finding a variety that is resistant to blight might be a good idea.

5. HARVESTING:

Once your plants have set four or five trusses of flowers/fruit, snip off the top of your plant. You now want it JUST to concentrate on ripening the remaining fruit.

If you do end up with a load of fruit that just won't turn from green to red at the end of the summer, pick them and stick them in a drawer with a banana, or leave them on a sunny windowsill. That usually works, though I think they do lose their flavour a bit. Or make green tomato chutney!

Pinch out the sideshoots

7. Salads

Now for some luscious salads! Rather than tomatoes, cucumbers and peppers, the focus here is on those lovely leafy or bulbous things that grow quickly and happily in containers of all sorts – hanging-baskets, patio pots, raised planters...you name it.

Of course, they can also be grown in greenhouses and conservatories, or outside once you're free of frosts. Lettuces, rocket, baby spinach, mustard and cress, beetroot, spring onions and radishes... Don't forget edible flowers – the peppery leaves and flowers of nasturtiums, marigold petals, viola flowers... All are generally easy and satisfying to grow.

1. SEED-SOWING:

Sow salad indoors in March in pots on a bright windowsill for early crops, or in April and May outdoors (late April onwards if you live in the North) in containers, growbags, raised beds, hanging-baskets – almost anything really as long as it has drainage holes.

Sprinkle your salad seeds thinly over the surface of moist, firmed compost. Some seed is very fine and will only need a very thin layer of compost, vermiculite or fine grit over the top; others like beetroot are a bit bigger and need a little more —about 1 inch (2.5cm). (Soak beetroot seed for a few hours before sowing).

Put the pots/trays somewhere bright and warm, but not too hot. Keep the compost/soil just moist while the seeds germinate, which should only be a matter of 10 days or so (it is VERY quick in the case of radishes!) If the soil is too wet, or you've sown the seed thickly, you may get problems with them all suddenly collapsing – 'damping off'. If this happens, salvage what seedlings you can and tuck them carefully into a different pot of compost, sow some more seed elsewhere and start again – it's just a small setback, and I promise you, every gardener's life is littered with those...

If you're sowing outside, choose a sheltered sunny place. Don't imagine they would look nice scattered all over the place. Baby salad leaves look practically identical to baby weeds – it becomes a nightmare to sort out! Make tiny shallow rows with a trowel, a dibber (or even a biro!) and sow your seeds into those, then cover them over. You'll easily be able to weed in between the rows when needed. Don't forget to label them.

Remember the plan is to keep your salad crops coming, so make a note to sow more seeds each week for a month or so. Another technique you could try is 'inter-planting' – popping these fast-growing things in between all sorts of other crops – radishes amongst the tatties or lettuces among the tomatoes. Onions like conditions a bit drier than most salad plants, but otherwise interplanted rows of growing crops work well and is a great way of using all available space.

Grow lettuces in rows

2. GROWING ON:

Once the little plants are coming up and big enough to get hold of, you need to 'thin' them – pull out ones that are growing very closely together so the remaining ones can develop better. Here's an admission – thinning is one of my most hated jobs in all of gardening! It feels so murderously wasteful to chuck away those little seedlings full of life and keen to grow, and I always curse myself for sowing them too thickly.

Salads like moist soil, but none of them need masses of fertiliser. Becoming dry is a common cause of 'bolting' – shooting up to flower – and that makes them much less palatable, with bitter leaves, etc. Cold weather can also trigger this. Your job is to deter them from doing their natural thing – flowering and setting seed – for as long as possible! Some plants, like mizuna and pak choi, prefer being sown later in the summer and there are bolt-resistant varieties of certain plants available, like beetroot 'Boltardy'. Sowing more seeds at regular intervals is your best insurance against losing a whole crop to climatic conditions.

Do watch out for slugs and snails – they

Shop-bought salad can't match the taste of homegrown

LOVE this stuff! Please only use safe organic controls – organic slug bait, beer traps, Sluggone mats, coffee grounds, creeping round late at night with a torch. They all work pretty well.

3. HARVESTING:

You can be harvesting baby leaves really quickly with these salad things – as soon as they look like the leaves you get in a supermarket bag of salad, snip some off for a lovely fresh-tasting lunch. As long as you don't damage the central growing point of the plant or take off ALL its leaves, it will keep growing. Young beetroot and radish leaves are also tasty. You should get at least three cuts off a plant before it's past its best. By that time, you should have more young plants coming along.

Lettuces that 'heart' up, like 'Iceberg' and 'Little Gem', take about three months from sowing, but you can start picking leaves from 'cut-and-come-again' (loose-leaf) varieties like 'Salad Bowl' from about seven weeks. Leaf mixes will also be ready at about seven weeks, radishes will be three to six weeks, beetroot about twelve weeks.

Radishes that have been growing happily in pots or rows in the veg plot can be harvested in as little as three to four weeks from sowing!

Beetroot – edible leaves, stem and root!

8. Courgettes and squashes

Courgettes and squashes are really good fun to grow if you have more than a shoebox of space.

I love getting so much PLANT from one seed. They are generally easy – even our horticulturally challenged little sister Caroline had roaring success with butternut squash last year! Just a couple of courgette plants will provide enough sweet, small courgettes for most families, I reckon.

1. VARIETIES:

There are dozens of varieties of both courgettes and squashes available. 'Defender F1' is a very well-known and reliable variety of courgette. If you're pushed for space or intending to grow courgettes in a container of some kind, 'Supremo' and 'Midnight F1' are good more compact choices. Or, how about courgettes with stripes – 'Zebra Cross F1', or bright yellow ones – 'Parador', for instance?

There are some really extraordinary and decorative squashes these days – 'Turk's Turban', 'Honeybear F1', 'Sunburst F1', 'Crown Prince', 'Hercules F1'… If you want to grow butternut squashes, but don't have loads of room, go for 'Butternut F1', and for an earlier crop than most, try 'Walnut F1'.

2. SEED SOWING:

Sow courgette and squash seeds either outside in late May-early June, where they are to grow, or March-April indoors to be planted out later once the danger of frost is past.

Most gardeners grow them in the ground or raised beds but if you're going to grow one in a container, it needs to be *big* – 18 inches (45cm) across at the top, at the VERY least, and preferably more – some of these plants can easily cover a square metre! Our brother grows them like this, to save them from pesky molluscs that like to shelter under the leaves. Having a bit of trellis or a fence and wires for the stems to scramble up might be a space-saving solution for the bigger squash varieties.

Outside, sow the big seeds very sparsely, 1 inch (2.5cm) deep in good fertilised soil. These plants really appreciate plenty of rotted manure, compost, and fertiliser. If you can, cover your seeds with upturned jars, or plastic bottles with the bottoms cut off to protect them and keep them a bit warmer until they've germinated. Once they've sprouted, pull out some to leave the remaining plants about 3 feet (1metre) apart.

Sow courgettes on their side

My preference is always to sow these seeds indoors and not too early, or they get enormous before the weather is OK for you to plant them outside!

Sow the seeds, one each to a small pot, 1/2 inch (1cm) deep into moist compost. Placing the seeds on edge is one way of preventing them rotting before they've germinated. Put the pots on a warm windowsill to germinate. Keep the soil damp but not wet.

3. GROWING ON AND HARDENING OFF:

After germination, courgettes and squashes grow quickly and will need to be put into a larger pot after three weeks or so. Try putting some compost in a larger pot. Set the pot with the plant in it down into the compost and make a 'pocket'. Then carefully tip out the seedling without disturbing its roots, pop it into the 'pocket' and fill it round with more compost. All done!

During May, put those grown inside, outside for increasingly long periods during the day, bringing them in at night for at least 10 days. Then plant them out at least 3 feet (1metre) apart in your veg bed or big container or Growbag. Sprinkle some seaweed or poultry-pellets over the whole area if you can.

These are thirsty plants and need *plenty* of watering, but try not to get the leaves wet.

Cold, damp weather will get fruiting off to a slow start. You may find the leaves develop white blotches or that the first few courgettes are a bit mouldy at the tips – I don't THINK it's just me! In my experience, neither of these things seems to make much difference to them later on. Take off any mouldy fruits or leaves you see, so that it doesn't spread, and keep watering the roots!

They would love some tomato fertiliser, especially the squash plants.

As they start to develop, try and support the courgette or squash fruits off the soil using a layer of straw, or perhaps a tile – it makes them less liable to rot and damage.

5. HARVESTING:

Once courgettes feel happy, the fruits come quickly! Do harvest them when they're small – 4-6 inches (10-15cm) at most – and that will keep them producing more. We had three plants last year and were picking them about three times a week! If you leave fruits on to develop into marrows, the plants will soon think their work is done, and stop producing any fruit at all. Cut the fruits off with a sharp knife rather than pulling them.

Squashes divide into two groups, summer and winter, and generally a summer squash like 'Sunburst F1' is harvested when the fruits are quite small, whereas butternut varieties, for instance, which are winter squashes, are left to develop longer on the plant and picked in autumn, for decoration or storing. With most, it doesn't make a lot of difference when you pick them, I don't think – just make sure you do it before the first frost hits!

Harvest squashes before the frosts

9. Winter veg

Let's fast forward to next winter: warming vegetable soups, vitamin-packed green leaf smoothies, crunchy homemade coleslaw and parmesan-encrusted roast parsnips with your Sunday lunch – YUM!

It may seem a world away, but actually spring is the right time to get cracking on the winter veg...

1. VEG CHOICES AND VARIETIES:

There's a huge choice of winter veg out there, from turnips to broccoli – here are some of our tried and tested favourites:

Cabbages – 'Greyhound' or 'Hispy' for those succulent pointy ones which will be ready to pick as early as July, followed by the exceptionally hardy 'January King' which will see you through the whole of the winter. Apparently we should all eat red and purple veg too, so try 'Red Flare' or the lovely sweet 'Kalibos' (perfect raw in winter salads).

Brussels sprouts – you can't go far wrong with 'Attwood' or 'Brodie'.

Leeks – 'Musselburgh' has been around for centuries and gives the volume of stem you need for soups but I'm also trying the slimmer 'Porbella' as well.

Parsnips – 'Gladiator' seems to have the right idea.

2. SOWING:

The three choices here:

Sow the seed indoors in trays, prick out into small pots, then bring the young plants on until they're ready to be transplanted into your veg patch (remember to 'harden off' though, like you do with courgettes etc).

Sow the seed directly into a nursery bed in your veg patch, then move them into a more spacious area when they have grown into young plants.

Buy the young plants at a stage when they can be popped straight out (slightly cheating but honestly no-one's judging).

Sowing the seed is straightforward but because so many winter veg come from the same family, brassica, seedlings look almost indistinguishable from each other so you must fervently label absolutely everything. You definitely won't be the first veg grower whose 'cabbages' suddenly start producing stems and Brussels sprouts. Tip from youngest sister Caroline: just pretend you knew that's what they were all along.

3. PLANTING:

For the first couple of months winter veg will be in seed trays, small pots or little nursery rows in your veg patch, so easy to manage, but when you move them to their permanent spots they

Leek seedlings – looks odd but this is correct

need a bit of room so you could be preparing a new veg bed or some large pots.

They're greedy things so now is the time to dig in any garden compost or manure, or, failing this, sprinkle in some balanced fertiliser from a packet. The only exception is for parsnips, which will 'fork' into several different roots if the ground contains manure, and they also do better if sown directly into where they are to grow and then thinned in the same way as carrots.

You should be ready to plant out your winter veg around the end of May/early June, after the last of the frosts.

Most books will tell you to plant them 3 feet (1metre) apart, but Laura's husband Tim says he's never planted anything more than 18 inches (45cm) apart, and leeks only 6 inches (15cm); at this closer spacing they'll just be smaller plants – what's the big problem?

Leeks need slightly different planting treatment to the others. First snip the top two inches off each plant then make cylindrical holes and drop each plant in, but don't firm the soil around it. Water thoroughly every day for around four days, until the roots have established at the bottom of the hole . The leek's stem will eventually bulk up and fill the hole.

Brussels sprouts will need a stake beside each plant as they start to develop their tall stem.

4. GROWING ON:

This is mostly straightforward maintenance of the bed, but humans are not the only species to enjoy eating brassicas. Whitefly, cabbage white caterpillars (the clue's in the name) and pigeons adore them too. The trick is to HAVE A PLAN. Be prepared so you're able to take each mini-invasion in your stride as if you were almost expecting them.

Whitefly. Fill a house-plant mister with a weak solution of washing-up liquid and spray plants every day for a week. The detergent kills the adult flies, but there will be a new batch hatching each day from eggs so you need to break the cycle.

Caterpillars. Just pick them off and feed them to the blue tits (harsh, but all part of your garden ecosystem). You may be able to intercept them at the egg stage – look for the little yellow clumps of them on the leaves and just squash them with your fingers.

Pigeons. You can try dangling CD discs on sticks around your crops but you may need further reinforcements in the form of netting.

5. HARVESTING:

Your outdoor veg patch or pot collection is simply the best fridge you could ever wish for, keeping your veg in tip-top condition until you need it. With careful management, crops such as leeks and parsnips might see you all the way through to the end of next March. And you could still have purple sprouting broccoli with your supper through the 'hungry gap' until the first of the spring crops are ready for harvesting.

Protect winter crops from pigeons!

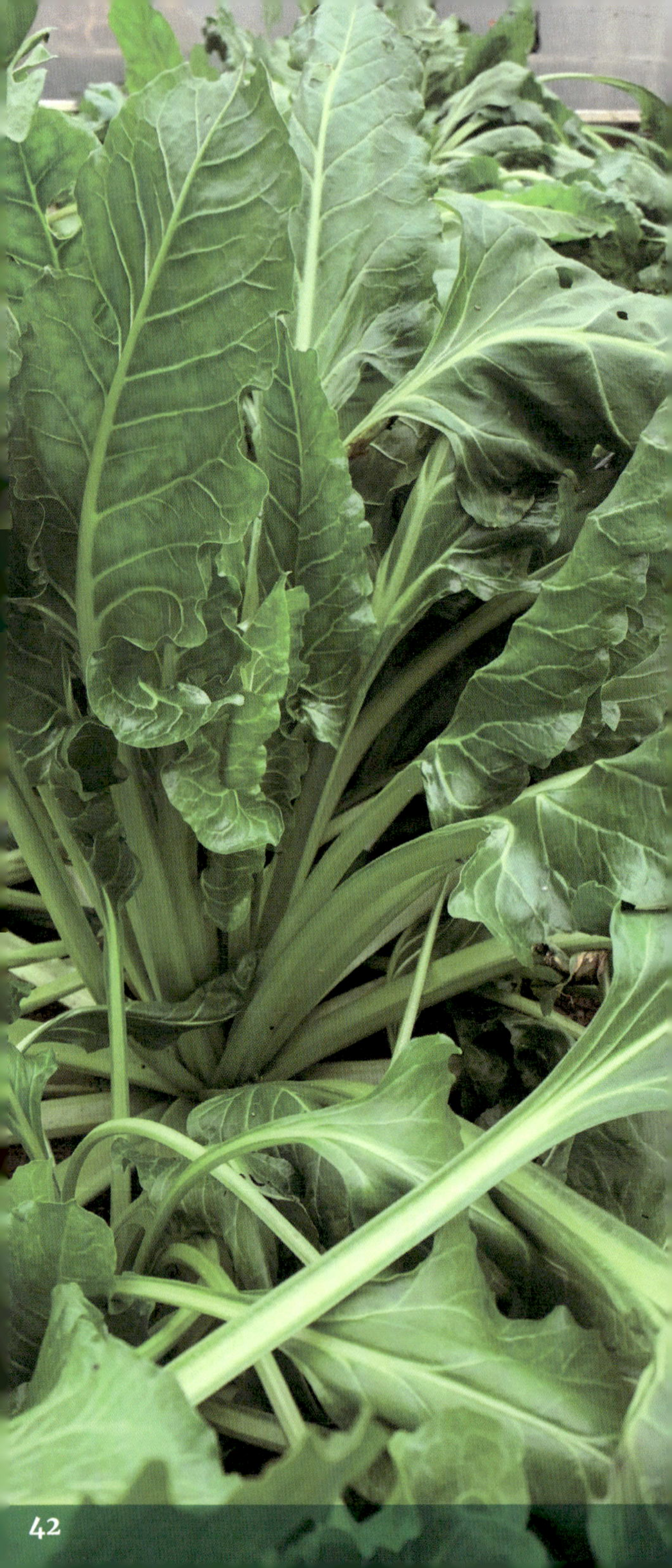

10. Chard, spinach and kale

How about some lovely leafy veg! Swiss chard, kale and spinach leaves are delicious and full of vitamins, whether cooked/steamed for stir-fries and the like, or eaten in salads when very young and fresh.

You can sow seeds of kale and chard throughout the spring and summer, and with a bit of protection, late-sown seedlings may even keep producing leaves for you through the winter if you can keep the pesky birds off them. Easy and attractive in pots, window-boxes and the flower-garden as well as in the veg plot, they're definitely worth a go.

1. PLANTS AND VARIETIES:

Lots of these kinds of veg plants are very pretty! There is a variety of chard called 'Bright Lights' that have a rainbow of stem colours – red, yellow, orange and pink.

'Ruby Chard' has glowing red stems and green leaves, 'Peppermint' has two-toned pink and white stems... They are definitely the thing to grow if you want your pots to be beautiful as well as productive. 'Dwarf Green Curled' is a good variety of kale for a windy spot like a balcony. The kale 'Nero di Toscana' with its big slate-coloured crinkled leaves looks and tastes amazing, though can be a bit of a 'diva', I find.

Spinach is a little bit trickier than chard or kale, at least for me – more prone to 'bolting' (shooting up to flower and thus spoiling the taste of the leaves), fungal disease (e.g 'downy mildew'), etc. Something called 'Spinach Beet' is easier for beginners, I would say, which doesn't have quite such a delicate flavour, but is less finicky in its habits.

2. SOWING:

These plants are tougher than a lot of annual veg. You can sow the seeds from March onwards into rows outside, pots of compost etc. 1 inch (2.5cm) deep and 2-3 inches (5-8cm) apart. Sun or slight shade is good. I use a bamboo cane along the row to make a very shallow trench. If you have more than one row, the rows should

Growing chard is worth it for the stems alone!

be about a foot (30cm) apart. Cover over the seed, water gently and make a mental note to sow a few more seeds in three weeks' time.

3. GROWING ON:

Once the little seedlings are coming up, you must 'thin' them out, pulling some out to leave the strongest to grow *at least* 8 inches (20cm) apart – a foot (30cm) if you want bigger plants that have less competition from their neighbours.

Mildew which manifests itself as white felty bits on the leaves and can cause the plants to collapse, is a bit of a pain sometimes – don't grow the plants too close together and try to water the soil around them, rather than on top of them. Remember, these plants are part of the 'brassica' family, and as such, are deeply appealing to marauding birds, especially pigeons. There are some suggestions for warding off these pests in the section on winter veg – good luck!

Keep the soil free of weeds and moist but not drenched. Since we want leaves and not fruit from these plants, a plant-feed containing more nitrogen rather than more potash, would be a great thing to water on the soil around them every two to three weeks, if you have such a thing. Keep the tomato fertiliser for plants that you want to encourage into flowering and fruiting.

If the plants become stressed in any way, they may 'bolt', so try to keep them evenly moist, weeded and happy. The weather can play a big part in this too. If they do start shooting up to flower, thus turning the foliage bitter and inedible, quickly dig up the whole plant and harvest what you can. At least you were very sensible and sowed more seeds a bit later, which will be absolutely FINE! (Hope is a marvellous thing – it's something most gardeners are very good at...)

4. HARVESTING:

As they grow, you can take off young fresh leaves from the outside of the plant for salads. They won't reach their full size until about three months after they were sown, but you can always take off a few to eat on the way. Cutting off individual leaves from the edge will prompt the plant to produce more of them in the middle – just the ticket.

One last thing – if you do want to grow chard and kale over the winter from September-sown seed, they will need a bit of protection (a greenhouse or a cloche, poly tunnel, horticultural fleece blanket, cosy mulch round the roots, closed cold frame, etc.) against the worst of the cold. Plants sown in July or August can be dug up carefully and grown on in a glassed-in entrance porch, perhaps?

They may stop growing in the depths of winter, but get going again next spring if they're feeling looked-after enough... and protected from the bloomin' pigeons!

Avoid mildew by watering the soil not the leaves

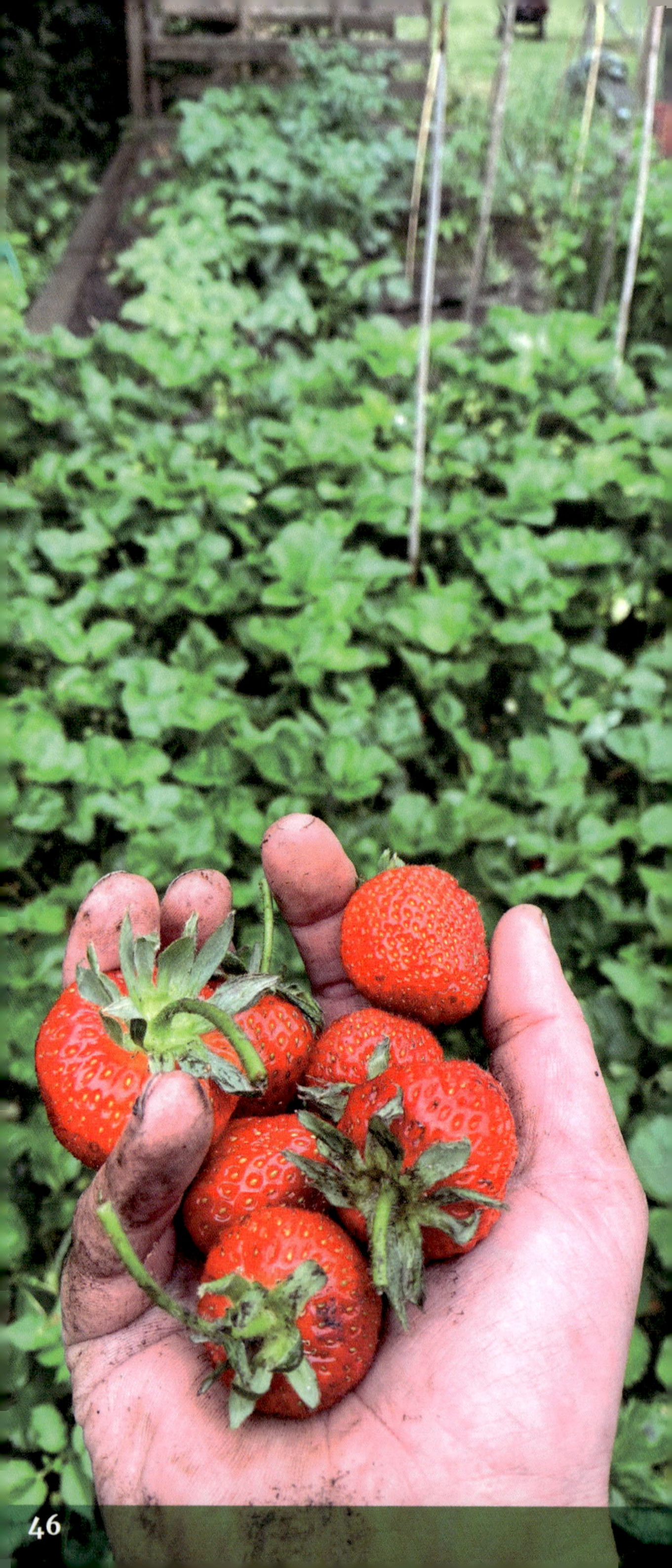

11. Fruit

If you're planning to grow your own veg, you might also be up for some fruit as well for delicious summer puds, jams and jellies, and a bit left over to stock up the freezer!

There's such a range of varieties now to suit any size of garden, terrace or even balcony. It's a huge topic so let's cut to the chase…

1. FRUIT BUSHES AND CANES:

If you're after maximising the produce from the space available, I would definitely prioritise fruit that tastes good fresh, but also freezes well. Nutritionists now tell us there is just as much goodness in frozen fruit and veg as eating it fresh. And remember by growing your own, you would be saving on all those 'food-miles' as well.

Raspberries, currants (black, red and white – they crop so heavily you probably only need one bush of each) and blackberries all score highly here.

Raspberries excel in cool summers and grow particularly well in Scotland. Try to get at least 10 canes to give you a decent crop. You're best planting them in a short row, so you can arrange posts and wires down either side to tie them into, to stop them flopping. I find the so-called autumn fruiting (actually late summer) kind the most productive, and easier to manage as you simply cut the lot to the ground each February.

Currant bushes need to be a good 4 feet (120cm) apart.

You can be more inventive with cultivated blackberries as they're from the bramble family, tough as old boots and happy to live life just scrambling over other things. They are also very attractive so don't be afraid to mix them in with other more ornamental stuff.

All these fruit bushes and canes are going to take a while to settle in and you may not get a great crop in the first year. But c'mon, all gardeners know the value of a bit of patience!

2. GROWING FRUIT IN POTS:

You can grow almost any sort of fruit in large pots nowadays, but they MUST be the right type. Fruit growers have selected varieties that are either genetically programmed to grow more compactly, or they've grafted normal-sized plants onto another much

Cut out the oldest stems of blackcurrant in winter

smaller variety of rootstock. Look out for the words 'dwarf' or 'patio' in front of the name and you know it's suitable to grow in a pot.

Blueberries are great in pots – you need at least two, as they prefer to cross-pollinate, and like acid soil so use 'ericaceous' compost. And finally have a plan to deter your friendly garden blackbirds around fruiting time, as they LOVE them.

3. STRAWBERRIES VERSUS RHUBARB:

You could have a bash at strawberries either in pots or in the open ground. They don't get properly into their stride until year three, after which you need to start again with some fresh young runners. That said, there's nothing like the smell and taste of a warm strawberry plucked straight from the plant!

A much more reliable option would be a patch of rhubarb, which you would be hard-pressed to get wrong, and gives a long season of sophisticated sweetness. Perhaps a kind neighbour who has an established clump could dig up a section for you? Shove this in a sunny corner and water it in well. Apart from the odd shovel of compost or manure, they require virtually no maintenance and will be providing you with sticks of rhubarb from next spring and for the next 20 springs thereafter.

4. CAN YOU GROW FRUIT FROM SEEDS?

Well, it's a mission. They rarely come 'true' from seed and you can waste several years growing on an inferior plant, but how about giving melons a try?

They do need a long hot summer to perform well, and probably the shelter of a cloche or greenhouse in northern gardens. You can grow them in an almost identical way to courgettes and squashes, but a month later because it really isn't warm enough to plant them out until mid- to late June.

Put them in your sunniest spot, and when they start flowering you can help the little melons to set by manually picking off a male flower and rubbing the pollen onto the female flower (they will have a more bulbous base than the male flower and are produced a little while after the male flowers get going).

5. FRUIT TREES:

Apple trees have the prettiest of all the blossoms but you'll need a second one, or another one in the neighbourhood, for good pollination to occur. They can also be tricky to store successfully. Even pears have only a very narrow window in which they're pleasantly soft yet still crisp and succulent to eat.

If I had to recommend just one fruit tree to grow in your garden it would be, by a country mile, a Victoria plum. Self-fertile (so you only need one) heavy cropping, and plums freeze beautifully – you just shove them in freezer bags.

Here's my recipe for cooking stewed plums from frozen: Step 1. Put them in the oven for 30 minutes. Step 2. Add sugar and cream. Step 3. Eat them. **DEE-licious!**

Victoria plum tree – a total winner!

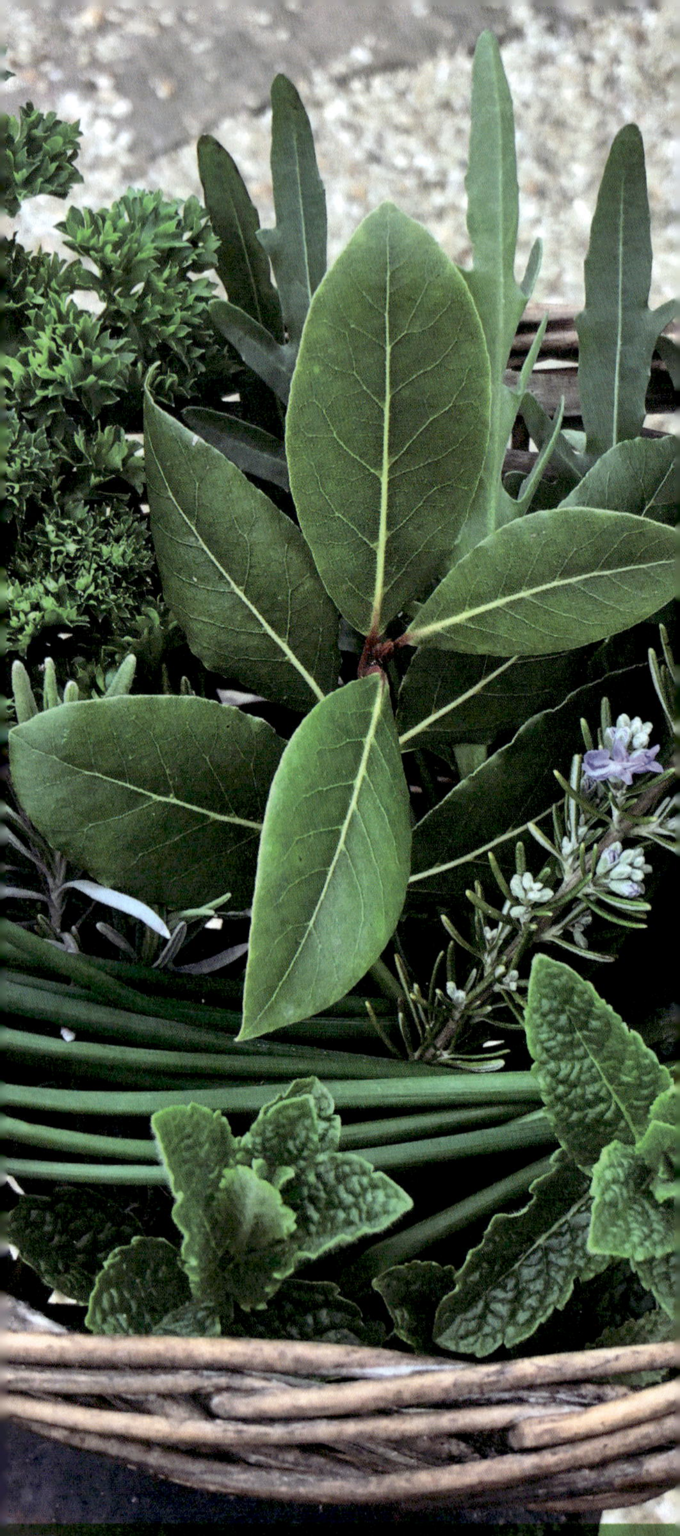

12. Herbs

Most herbs are a cinch to cultivate (hurray!) and they're just as great for containers, hanging baskets, planters, balcony windowboxes, planting pockets on a wall or trellis, etc as they are for a pretty little herb garden by the back-door, or edging for a path or veg bed...

1. PLANTS AND VARIETIES:

Herbs can be annuals (start, flower and die in one season) e.g. basil, dill, coriander; biennials (start in one year, flower and die the next year) e.g. parsley, chervil; or perennials (come up year after year) e.g. chives, fennel, sage, mint, tarragon, lavender, thyme, marjoram.

Bay is a common 'tree-herb', which can be topiarised to keep it neat, and rosemary makes a pretty, scented shrub that really attracts pollinating insects.

Almost all of these have lots of different named varieties, including some interesting and lovely-sounding things like 'Eau de Cologne' mint and 'Red Boza' basil, but the basic species ones are great to grow too. Coriander 'Leisure' or 'Cilantro' are less likely to bolt (run up to flower and seed) than the ordinary kind, but you can also eat the yummy green seeds! Dill 'Nano' is good for pots or smaller spaces, being bushier and more compact than others.

By the way, if you buy supermarket herbs to grow on, do be very careful – they have been deliberately grown to produce fabulous lush leaves, but their roots may be very weak – they may need a lot of TLC to coax them into being good garden plants.

2. SOWING:

Sow the seeds of basil, chives and parsley indoors in pots or trays of compost on a sunny windowsill. Parsley prefers things a bit warmer, if you can manage it. Our Dad had plastic containers of parsley seeds germinating in moist tissue paper above the old coal-fired Aga...

Sprinkle them thinly over moist compost, cover them with a fine layer of compost, vermiculite or grit and leave to germinate. When handling fine seed, one tip is to put some seeds into a piece of folded paper and tap the paper gently as it you move it over the surface of the compost.

Herbs are basically sun-lovers, preferring a light, well-drained soil. Try and dig in some grit or sand if your soil is full of thick clay. They might appreciate some well-rotted manure or compost dug into the soil before planting, if possible, but don't go bonkers with that. Remember most come from the Med, and don't need or like rich or soggy soil.

Tap out fine seeds from a fold of paper

Some such as coriander, chervil, parsley or mint are OK in a shadier situation. In fact, mint can go even more crazy in shade than it does in sun – be careful! Though wonderful for cooking, mint is a rampant colonizer. I grow it in a pot sunk into the herb garden so it doesn't take over the whole area, and just make sure it doesn't dry out.

Coriander, dill and chervil can be sown outdoors where they are to grow, from March onwards. And since these grow rapidly, it's a great idea to sow some more in a couple of weeks – and maybe some more a couple of weeks after that! Again sow the seeds thinly and no more than an inch deep.

Once the inside seedlings have germinated, pot them up into individual modules, and gradually 'harden them off' by leaving them outside during the day, and bringing them inside at night. A tip about parsley – it gets grumpy about being transplanted, so sow two to three seeds into individual pots from the get-go, and plant the whole potful out as a unit.

It's very important to do this hardening off process with herb-plants bought from the supermarket too.

Plant them out into sunny positions in late April or May, in raked fine soil which you've already watered.

3. GROWING ON:

Keep the plants watered well until they're growing strongly. After that, twice a week (into the soil not over the plants themselves) should be fine. In fact, some gardeners believe you should keep herbs starved and thirsty, in order to get the best flavour from them. I'm sure a happy medium can be struck, and is certainly easier on the eye! They are also more likely to 'bolt' if they're bone-dry.

Herbs are easy to maintain on the whole. Pinch out the tips of basil stems to make the plants bushier. Trim back thyme lightly after it's finished flowering. Cut back the flowers of perennial herbs in summer to encourage new leaves, especially the spent flower-stems of lavender.

4. HARVESTING:

You can be picking rocket, coriander or dill as soon as three weeks after sowing the seed!

When picking your herbs, it helps to take leaves from the outside of the plant to encourage new leaves to grow in the centre, and some gardeners reckon they are fuller of their essential oils in the morning than at other times of day.

If you get a glut, you can freeze herbs (what about filling an ice-cube tray with herbs in water?) or dry them. At the end of the summer, you can pot up chives, parsley, mint etc. to bring indoors to pick sparingly through the winter to liven up your dishes.

Herbs like this sage will yield easy cuttings

Index

Beetroot	33
Broad beans	15
Brussels sprouts	39
Cabbages	39
Carrots	25
Chard	43
Chitting	11
Companion planting	9
Courgettes	35
Creating bed	7
Damping off	31
Dwarf runner beans	23
Earthing up	12
Fruit	47
Hardening off	23, 36
Herbs	51
Kale	43
Labelling	9
Leeks	39
Lettuce	31
Onions	19
Parsnips	39
Peas	24
Potatoes	11
Radishes	33
Salads	31
Seed-sowing	9
Shallots	19
Spinach	43
Squashes	35
Tomatoes	27
Watering	8
Weeding	8
Winter vegetables	39